Pristine Moments, Lucid Dreams

Select Memoirs of Young Cebuano Voices

Edited by

Manu Avenido

Ukiyoto Publishing

Foreword

It is a little past seven on a Monday morning and the rain has just stopped outside. I count this as an auspicious start to the week. Today, this bubble of reflection shields me somehow from the minute and immediate worries I would otherwise have if I had gone on today the way I did with my other Mondays.

This is precisely the gift that this book gives us: a chance to do what Susan Lara calls "living life twice," with all its pain and beauty, and to glean from it something we can take to steel or soften us for the next moment. These young Cebuano writers have taken it upon themselves to write about the concepts that intrigue them, the ideas, things, and people around which their lives revolve: be it religion, love and friendship with the creatures around us, family conflict, physical and mental sickness, the act of writing itself, or death. There is nothing trivial here: even the humble *humba* gets to take its rightful place in our pantheon of core memories, as Pixar's *Inside Out* terms these enduring and valuable moments, no matter how bittersweet they are.

It is such a pleasure to know that these piercing insights come from young but kindred spirits, with sharp senses attuned not only to the physical aspects of life, but also to its innate contradictions. Our young writers have bridged the anguish of silence into articulation and mapped not just a part of their personalities but also their positionality, as Cebuanos, as young people of today. More than just being a record of pivotal moments, this book is an assertion of the truth of lived experiences, a testament of moments of attention leading to self-questioning and into understanding.

I also laud the editor for his keen eye, something the best teachers have, in seeing in these essays the beginnings of an examined, and therefore much-lived life, once in experience, and the second time, in writing. Manu Avenido clearly has what Dr. Marjorie Evasco terms as "compassionate understanding," honoring the stories of his students and giving them space to breathe. This is a difficult undertaking and may even take a toll on teachers of CNF, but this is also another way for us to walk with our students and connect with them not just as teachers but as fellow humans with similar griefs and joys. With the refreshing honesty and vulnerability of the intensely personal, what Philippe Lejeune calls the "autobiographical pact" is fulfilled, and it is now our turn as readers to safeguard and cherish these stories as if they were our own.

This book invites us to sift through our lives and have an epiphany, yes, even for breakfast. It ends with tentativeness, even hope, for good things ahead even as we learn from experience and memory. So before I give in to my calendar reminders of tasks (it *is* a Monday, after all), before we go forward with our lives, let us take this moment of conscious attention and self-reflection.

There is something here for everyone. *Ali na, magbasa ta!*

Carmie Ortego

Metro Manila, Philippines

September 12, 2022

Preface

The short memoirs included in this collection are 14 of the best outputs of my talented senior high school students in my Creative Nonfiction class last 2018. The book was initially launched at the 1st Yamog ArtFest of our Humanities and Social Studies (HUMSS) Department held in the same year.

Each memoir piece was written as briefly as 2,000 words or less by these young, promising writers who, even if they wrote commendable English, were certainly not detached from their identity as Cebuanos. In fact, their voices amplified by their own unique and significant life experiences resonate greatly those of most Cebuano millennials. It is this important aspect of their writing that I, as editor, have paid careful attention to as I ensured to preserve the authenticity in their voices.

The book is divided into two parts: *Pristine Moments* and *Lucid Dreams*. The first half is a recollection of the writers' most precious memories growing up—so precious that they have remained to them palpable until now. The latter half will bring the readers to each writer's reverie or introspection, which even though they seemed to be in some sort of a trance or daydreaming, a sense of clarity for themselves was still found.

It is with great pride that I present this humble collection, which I think is first of its own as far as Cebuano Literature is concerned. May this book inspire more HUMSS teachers and students in our country and all CNF lovers to take the same path. May this be the first of many opportunities for our young voices to be heard.

Acknowledgments

The editor wishes to express his gratitude to the following:

Carmie Ortego, for the Foreword of this book

Jude Ortega and Haidee Palapar, for the blurbs

Josua Cabrera, for the cover art

Kei Saito, Kyla Sophia Abatayo, Shanika Marie Lumayno, and Brenzy Kaye Maquilan, for the illustrations

All Grade 12 HUMSS students of the University of San Jose-Recoletos Batch 2018, for sharing their stories in and outside the book

Contents

Introduction

An Abundance of True Bare Selves

"For out of the abundance of the heart his mouth speaks."
Luke 6:45

If there is one thing this humble book promises to the readers, it is not the vain ambition to offer memoirs as lucrative and masterful like that of seasoned, professional writers. Rather, what this book hopes to bring is the undeniable amount of talent and dedication to the craft of memoir writing each of the 14 young Cebuano contributors ardently showed in their maiden works.

There is nothing grand and imposing in this collection. There is only the downright sincerity and openness, and the unpresuming bravery to reveal and share some human experiences as trivial as watching the rain with glee or as profound as pondering upon one's own existence. It is altogether generous and courageous for the featured writers here to examine their young lives and expose their vulnerability to others. For it is in this moment where they are at their most vulnerable, when they let their guards down and reflect, that they get to reconcile and know themselves more deeply.

2

Kate Alimpolos' *Being Lost in My Own Hometown* welcomes the readers as she reminisces some precious memories of her hometown—the mango tree where she and her friends used to climb and play, her grandfather's chicken coop, and the wafting aroma in her grandmother's kitchen. It is in this particular moment in Kate's recollection where she shows her most vulnerable, her most bare self:

> I wish I had never grown up. It was just
> too sudden. It feels as if it was only
> yesterday when I had no worries. I could
> look back and have no regrets. I didn't
> feel as if I had to satisfy someone for it to
> be okay to be me.

Certainly, no matter how long she has been away from her town, her childhood memories will always be the compass guiding her back home. This sentimental act of relating memory of place, home, and people to things with significant value is also manifested in Robert John Medida's *Tuesdays with My Mother's Humba* and Jewil Anne Tabiolo's *The Night-Blooming Jasmine.*

Robert John, who confesses he was a stubborn son to his mother as he took his studies for granted back then, recounts the moment he saw her in the hospital—a pivotal moment in his life, "I felt the world sinking beneath my feet. My tears cascaded in an endless river of loneliness and pain as I saw my mother on a wheelchair with her left leg wrapped with bandages due to some wounds and bruises." Like

Kate, Robert John is always drawn back to his hometown and his mother as he relishes this famous Filipino dish—the *humba*. But more than this dish, what he actually craves for all these years is his mother's love:

> A mother is irreplaceable as she is the person who can love us genuinely. In her special homemade recipe that suits my taste well, it is a blessing to experience her *savory* love. Every Tuesday, I remember two things which have made me who I am today—my mother and her *humba*.

One can only marvel at an unblinking wisdom in Robert John's memoir that there can still be a deep worth even in the typical and the familiar, in the ordinary and the usual, like a homemade dish, or the seasonal flowers that Jewil used to see blooming in her grandmother's garden when she was younger. In her memoir, she deftly compares herself to the Dama de Noche as she unlocks some family secrets that would later on explain the kind of personality she has–recluse and self-effacing.

Such discovery wouldn't have been arrived at had she not mustered up the courage to share some pristine bittersweet moments and reveal her bare self through her story. Just like Robert John and Jewil who find comfort in each of their family, Shyamelissa confidently expresses in her memoir *Balay-Laaganan* her sense of rootedness and belongingness in the

4

confines of her home, through the loving, reassuring presence of her OFW (overseas Filipino worker) mom. All the lures of the outside world pale in comparison to the joy and satisfaction she gets inside their abode for as she says, "When my mom is here, our house would feel more of a home."

Perhaps, the boldest attempt at exposing someone's vulnerability belongs to Janine Chilo Chin's *A Beautiful Mistake* and Shanika Marie Lumayno's *War-Torn*. No braver act there can be than revisiting some sad, painful episodes in our life like in Janine's work, or battling against invincible foes inside our heads like in Shanika's piece.

Jeanne Heredia's ~~Confined~~ brings us to the core of her vulnerability as she contemplates on her very own existence while lying in her hospital bed alone, succumbing to her illness and enduring some irksome feeling of restlessness and claustrophobia:

> The loneliest thing that might happen to you when you are being hospitalized is celebrating your birthday in your room. Not being able to eat chocolate cake and ice cream because I couldn't consume dark colored food, and simply not being able to eat because of zero appetite. Even looking at the food on the TV screen made me want to puke. It was miserable hating something that I loved so much.

Her state of confinement for several days and the feeling of displacement as a result thereof has led her to a deeper understanding of her own groundedness and ultimately, her own existence. For it is at times when we lose our bearings that we have to pause and recollect in order to journey inside. And it is when we take hold of our interiority that we connect more meaningfully with the people around us, as gleaned in Devey Joy Gaviola's piece *Passionately Drunk on Writing*:

> I made a set of resolutions of trying new liquors, writing different genres of literature. The next time I would write, it would not only mirror my sentiments but of people. It would not be my truth, but the truth that everyone should know. Someday, I would pen a book that would create happiness and ignite inspiration to others. I wanted to take away the loneliness of the people that once mirrored mine.

Karen Belocura's *Growing Up with the Augustinian Recollect Emblem* may also resonate to the idea of understanding one's self in order to relate with others, but this time, it is the other way around. This moment of introspection was prompted by her junior high teacher, in the midst of a most pressuring circumstance, in the abundance of her teacher's true bare self rebounding to hers:

> At that time, I found the Augustinian Recollect emblem in her. In her, I found rest. In her, I saw the flaming heart

pierced by an arrow. I saw it in her as she led us back to knowing ourselves. I saw it in her when she reminded us that we don't necessarily have to reach the standards of other people and we shouldn't seek their validation.

Brenzy Maquilan's *The History of You and Me: Through Reversed Time* speaks of the vulnerability of the human heart in the abundance of love. In her piece she celebrates the exuberance of her young, carefree love. It is through our innate human capability to share our affection to others, heedless of the possible circumstances, that we do not only become more compassionate and selfless, but we also become wiser.

Such vulnerability in the gripping force of love is also shown in Pamela Ceciban's *Wayward Currents* and Matiz Erika Lumapas' *Dead Leaves*. Pamela narrates how her relationship with her OFW father during her younger years started fragile and unavailing since she grew up without his presence. But when she opened up herself, and allowed her true bare self to glow, all the walls between them came crumbling down:

> We grew closer to each other and I realized that I somehow got most of my mannerisms and the way I think things through from him. I also found out that we resemble the way he sees life and the way I see it. We have way many more similarities than I thought.

Matiz, on the other hand, has been trying to reconnect with her long lost friend up until now. Attending to the demands of her teenage life, she has been perplexed by some scattered memories through the clutter in her room that keeps haunting her:

I had an urge to dive under my bed and discover everything hidden in the dark depths of dust, and to climb up into the highest corners of my closet and recover items that had been mingling with the spider webs. The innocent piles were growing higher and higher until they looked tarrying in my eyes. It's as if the spiders were threatening to swallow me whole. I had to get rid of them.

But no matter how much she wants to get rid of some old, almost-forgotten memories, like those of her lost friend, she will never contain the overwhelming longingness she's been enduring through these years unless she clears up herself not only from the clutter in her room, but most importantly, from all the mess inside her.

We are also placed at a similar position in Lance Roi Catadman's *Blue Rain* and Samantha Tabotabo's *Ignacio* where both recollect their friendship—the former with a childhood friend, the latter with a cat. Both are self-confessed pluviophiles or lovers of rain. Lance's reminiscence, almost like a lucid dream, while watching rain inside a jeepney in the middle of the traffic and flood, has transported him to some rarely unvisited recesses of his memory, including that of his childhood friend. Such act of reverie has led him to appreciate this life's essential reality:

> I realized that we are all in one with the rain. We are all droplets of different stories. Each of us gives meaning to this life we have, just like how the rain gives life to the earth.

After reading Samantha's piece, we could surely feel the double-edged truth piercing through our hearts. Motivated by the gravity of pain and anger she felt after her dear cat, the animal she regarded as her best friend, was killed by a seemingly-unapologetic kid in their neighborhood, she was struck by a realization one time that would definitely change her perspectives about life, death, and friendship:

> Maybe the child does not understand the concept of death, that she is simply too young to discern that her actions could take the life of another. All of that was beyond her understanding.

All contributors in this collection are young writers who have to deal with growing up, family and friends, school works, internal battles, fragile loves and heartaches, and life's demands as teenagers. There's really nothing grand and imposing here. But each of the memoirs in this book speaks of wide-eyed truths and openhanded willingness of these promising writers to share their genuine selves at their most vulnerable. For there is strength in vulnerability. For there is honesty in the abundance of true bare selves.

May you enjoy this labor of love.

Manu Avenido

Cebu City, Philippines

March 13, 2018

Pristine Moments

Being Lost in My Own Hometown

Kate Eloiza Alimpolos

We have our own unforgettable childhood memories. Memories buried deep into our hearts. Childhood is a time when we are influenced by incidents that will remain with us in our entire lives. As for me, my childhood was the best memory I have, mainly because I was surrounded by people who guided, encouraged, and believed in me.

The Mango Tree

It was every summer vacation when my friends and I would always visit this mango tree at the back of our house. This mango tree stood tall through the years, and had also survived many typhoons. Every morning my friends and I would go and climb up that mango tree where each of us owned a branch we could sit on and called it our home. We would carve our names on the branches so that no one could take our place in that mango tree we dearly loved.

Apart from the fun and excitement that we felt every time we climbed it, we also loved the scenery we could see from the mango tree like the overlooking view of the sea and the vacant lot covered with green Bermuda grass. But as much as we loved to be in the mango tree all day, my Uncle Dodong wouldn't allow us. We always got scolded for climbing up that tree. Stubborn as we were, we never listened. We would still climb the tree the following day, and the next day, and the day after next.

It became a cycle. Early morning with our pajamas still on, we were already climbing up the mango tree, sitting and treating it as our house. Then Uncle Dodong would pass by. He would look up the tree and find us. He would then snap a stem of *malunggay* nearby, rip its leaves off, and use them to shoo us away. And then it was our cue. Terrified of our Uncle Dodong, we would climb down from the tree screaming and laughing at the same time.

The Chicken Coop

When I was young, I loved visiting my Lolo Ani's chicken coop. I loved helping him feed his chickens, collect the eggs, and put them in an incubator until they hatch in the following weeks or so. Back then I was never the girly type. I had long hair but never bothered combing it. I found comfort in wearing simple shirts and pants rather than fancy dresses. And helping my Lolo in his chicken coop was the only fun thing I knew at the tender age of 7.

On Sundays, my Lolo would often bring me to the cockpit arena in town. And there, I could see a lot of people—all loud and noisy. Back then, I didn't know what a cockpit arena was. All I knew was that it was the place where my Lolo would go whenever he was bored and wanted to be entertained. After going to the cockpit arena, we would go home secretly because my mother hated the idea of me being with my Lolo in that place. I did not complain about that. I got my mother's point. Since then, I have had this close bond with my Lolo. Whenever I see a chicken coop, I would beam a smile silently remembering what it felt like going into one.

My Lolo passed away many years ago. But the memories of him and his chicken coop will never fade. They have just taken a new form. Because even though they are memories of a child, even if I've changed roles in life over the years, they have become a part of the person I am today.

Nanay Marly's Kitchen

My most favorite place has always been my Nanay's house. This is the place I would have to go to before and after school. I have always loved my Nanay's house because it made me feel safe and warm. There was the aroma of coffee in the air at all times. It seemed like all my Nanay did was to make coffee. If I smell coffee now, I instantly think of my Nanay Marly's house. I didn't know how old my Nanay was. "Old" was an abstract thing for a seven-year-old. I only knew that she was a lot older than my dad, who in my memory was pretty old. But obviously age had something to do with smell, because things just smelled differently at my Nanay's house. You could expect me to recollect memories of the special aroma of freshly-baked bread or some other pleasant smell.

I suppose that is why I remember it being such a special treat to go to Grandma's during the holidays. Her kitchen was in full production in those special times. Missing the experience of her kitchen, I could only reminisce today about the times that we gathered as a family. When we left, the smell of her delicious food would slowly fade in our smell, and the last thing we would see was my Nanay waving at us through the window, leaving me a warm, comforting feeling. I would look up into the dark night sky as we drove our way home, and think of all the fun cooking experiences I had there with my Nanay.

I wish I had never grown up. It was just too sudden. It feels as if it was only yesterday when I had no worries. I could look back and have no regrets. I didn't feel as if I had to satisfy someone for it to be okay as me. Life is full of responsibilities. Homework. Fights. Grades. Parents. Being a teenager. When I was little, the future was so far ahead I didn't care about what I wanted to be when I grew up. "I could think about that later," I would say. Now, everything is so close. We didn't even realize the journey we've been through. We were just living. The world we knew has lost its innocence. And it has gotten colder. Colder than I could remember. Our eyes have opened. As soon as you grow older, it's not the same. People around you want to suit you to their costumes and turn you into one of them.

The funny thing is, for over the years, many have come and go. Many things stayed as they were, but more things have also changed. What was left are only the memories. The rest of them have vanished. The mango tree that we used to climb back when we were still kids was cut down because the lot was used to build a house. The chicken coop that served as a sanctuary for both me and my Lolo is now unattended. After my Lolo passed away, no one cared to preserve the very one place he cared about. My Nanay's kitchen is still existing, but the very person who could make that kitchen come to life has now led to a different path. I guess there are things that no matter how hard we want it to happen again or wish to go back to that very moment, it is still not for us to decide.

I have been living independently in the city for quite some time now, but whenever I come home, these childhood memories would always cross my mind. How simple was life then! How people played a vital role in each other's life!

If only I had a remote control for life, I would go back to the good times, forward the sad and relive the awesome episodes, and pause the moments that are slipping through my fingers. But time won't stop. Time doesn't wait for anyone. That's what memories are for. Surely, some memories may not be as happy as others, but they are proof that I have lived. Memories will be with us forever. To teach, to remind, and to show us that growing up is part of life.

One is born, grows up, and dies. That's how it is. That's how it will always be.

Growing Up with the Augustinian Recollect Emblem

Karen Claire Belocura

1. *Augustinian Recollect Emblem*

The Augustinian Recollect emblem serves as an identity to the members of the Order of Augustinian Recollects (OAR). It is a figure of a flaming heart pierced with an arrow. More than its artistic appearance, this emblem signifies a deeper value and belief. The flaming heart represents the burning passion of St. Augustine to know God more, for he believes that in knowing God, an individual also gets to know himself more. This also symbolizes St. Augustine's love for God and for his brothers and sisters. On the other hand, the piercing of the flaming heart with an arrow symbolizes the restlessness of St. Augustine that led him to find true rest in God.

For the last six school years of my stay at the University of San Jose–Recoletos, I have been constantly taught to live by the meaning of this emblem. In some way, I found myself attached to this emblem. In a lot of ways, I grew up keeping this emblem close to my heart.

Almost all of the time, this emblem is my only source of strength when I feel restless due to school requirements. In some instances, when I have to stay late at night trying to understand every arithmetic expression written on thick pages, or when I have to set my tiny fingers in pressing some characters overnight because I will face an oh-so-bright panel the following day, I just have to remember the meaning of this emblem. I know who and where to find strength and rest from. By this, I can truly say that this emblem is what makes me move forward and what makes me survive the hardships that I face in my stay in this institution.

2.   *St. Augustine*

Almost, if not all, know St. Augustine as the man from Thagaste who used to be full of vices, and someone who used to be described as "worldly," but was later on converted when he found rest in God. This may be true, but every time I hear "St. Augustine," I always think of forty-three girls in a button-down collared garment with a green-colored jumper. The reason behind this perception of mine is because St. Augustine is also a section in University of San Jose–Recoletos. In junior high, this section is considered the cream of the crop of the girls' high school.

In my entire junior high school years, all I was aiming for was to be part of this section beginning from Grade 8 until Grade 10 only since pilot sections do not exist in Grade 7. In order for Grade 7 students to get into the St. Augustine section when they reach Grade 8, they have to earn specific grades during the fourth quarter. On the other hand, students in the upper year level who already belonged to St. Augustine have to maintain their grades in order to earn their keep.

I don't know if it was pure luck, a blessing, or probably both, but I was able to land into this section when I turned Grade 8. Needless to say, I never planned to be attached with anyone, not even a single person from this section, since it had always been hard for me to say goodbye, and I always had difficulty moving on. I was a hundred percent sure that all I ever wanted was to try the life of being a student from a pilot section. However, in life, someone doesn't just give in to everything he or she wants. Grade 8 was just the start of everything. It had not yet even reached the tip of the iceberg.

Fortunately, I was able to remain in St. Augustine when I reached Grade 9. That time, especially when August 2014 came, the tables had finally turned. It has always been a culture of the University of San Jose–Recoletos Junior High School Department to hold different activities for each grade level to celebrate the *Buwan ng Wika* or National Language Month. For Grade 9 students, *Katutubong Sayaw* (folk dance) was our main activity. It was a competition, and all sections were enjoined from participating. It's also a given fact that all students of all sections must have a task—either as a dancer or as a propsperson. Since we were considered as the cream of the crop, the pressure of winning was always with us. I can still clearly remember when our class, led by Reinette, was assigning tasks to everyone. We were all keen on choosing our dancers since their performance was the most crucial part. One wrong move, and everything became topsy-turvy—everything was going to fail. Because the decisions we take can always make or break our future. As for me, I automatically volunteered to be a propsperson. I mean, I had no intention of destroying our performance. Dance was never made for me. Even the waves and the wind can boast to me that they are more graceful than I am.

Looking at the list of our assignments, I was confident that we would be able to do more than good. However, something must be done in order to achieve this. Hence, despite having a lot of performance tasks and the impending first quarter exam, we allotted a lot of time for practicing and making props. It started out well. However, pressure started to build up more and more as time passed by, especially when the day for the eliminations was getting closer. Our Saturdays and holidays were stolen from us. In those days, I would hear the clacking of those long hollow stems as I saw them being carried from school to my classmate's house where we used to practice and make props when the school was unavailable. Huge plastic bags with colorful papers of crumpled surface and circular polystyrene kept appearing in front of me as if they were children waiting for their parents to be molded for them to become better individuals.

Pressure was always building up every minute. At that time, our homeroom teacher, Ms. Delfin, sat with the propsmen and helped us in making the sunburst prop. Though we seemed relaxed and happy, she knew that deep inside us was the burden of meeting the standards and expectations of the people around us. When we heard words of stones thrown into the air, she immediately went to the dancers to ease the tension between them. She then told us that meeting the expectations of everyone was not all that mattered. Trophies and certificates don't attest to true winning. Rather, it is by growing up and becoming a better individual through our experiences.

At that time, I found the Augustinian Recollect emblem in her. In her, I found rest. In her, I saw the flaming heart pierced by an arrow. I saw it in her as she led us back to knowing ourselves. I saw it in her when she reminded us that we don't necessarily have to reach the standards of other people and we shouldn't seek their validation. Our relationship as sisters was far more important than anything else. We realized the true meaning and purpose of all our efforts. And in that very moment, our friendship turned into sisterhood. We found faith in each other. It was also when I found the heart-warming attachment that I used to hate.

3.   *Ambition*

Belonging in a pilot section, it was a given that I was surrounded with individuals thriving in an ambitious environment. Then again, people expected us to devour each other and race against each other towards the throne. However, that was not the case. The truth was, truly we were in an environment of competition—competition between ourselves only. We are 24/7 ready to help, support, and cheer for each other. It was our joy to see our sisters getting what they wanted. At the same time, it was our sorrow when we saw our sisters feeling disappointed in themselves.

Although everyone was aiming for excellence, the competition was set within ourselves. We even reviewed our exams together. I remember one December, when everyone's eyes were heavy and droopy, and nobody wanted to hold their pens and work on anything. With my hair all over my face and my head throbbing, I was cramming to understand every single lesson in our Math subject for our upcoming periodical exam. Fortunately, our top student, who happened to be my seatmate, came to teach me all those lessons. Rather than becoming an opponent, seeing our sisters achieve what they wanted had become our common ambition.

Having this kind of attitude must be a product of growing up with the Augustinian Recollect emblem. Choosing to ignite our hearts full of pressure and uncertainties with the fire of respect and love for God and for others. Piercing one's heart with humility won't hurt after all. Instead, it brings satisfaction and rest. Besides, I believe that the best ambition that I could ever dream of is to know myself by trusting God and by securing the welfare of other people around me.

Tuesdays with My Mother's *Humba*

(With apologies to Mitch Albom)

Robert John Medida

I don't know why Tuesdays and eating *humba* make me remember so many old memories. It is funny how this day and this food can gather together all the lost time inside my head. Every bite is like partaking an old memory and every sip of its sauce can transport me back to that special time. I'd like to think that its savor and taste has been responsible for what I have become today.

I was walking back to the house under the dark clouds one Tuesday afternoon. Its cheerless wind mirrored my mood. It was almost six o'clock in the evening when I finally arrived at my destination. There was a deafening silence inside the house, except for the chirping of insects outside, while I waited for my mother to come home. I was excited for dinner. Although it was a market day, arriving home later than five o'clock was unusual for her. She would signal a yell to my other siblings to fetch her from the road and help her carry the stuff she was bringing.

However, that Tuesday was different from all the other Tuesdays in the past. As I lit the lamp, Nong Cesar arrived in our *kubo* and informed us that our mother was rushed to the hospital for the reason he didn't know. Upon hearing the news, it seemed like I was under a cloud that kept growing darker and darker. My pulse quickened, my breathing became heavy, and my spine shivered brought by the cold wind. I had so many unanswered questions arising in my mind as I was choked with intense emotions.

In a quaint town of Boljoon, in the southern part of Cebu, people have a simple life. That includes us who just go to the town once a week to sell our crops and other farming produce to other villagers. They also use it as a shopping day. My mother used to sell *bibingka* in the market as people were busy having their one-day shopping, strolling around in the *ukay-ukayan*, playing volleyball, and the most common thing of all, eating *pansit* at Noy Rofu's Carenderia.

After folks from the mountain purchased their one-week supply of goods, they would ride in Nad-Nad's truck which was as old as the driver— almost some of its parts seemed to give up. Despite the truck's appearance, it could still cater around thirty to fifty passengers, including the sacks of rice and other supplies. It was an old truck painted in green to look fresh to the eyes despite its old design. Passengers also used to ride on the truck's roof in order to reach back to their place. It was always around four thirty in the afternoon when the truck would reach the local basketball court in Barangay Lunop near our school, which served as a terminal for people to get off. We used to hitch in the truck as it went back to the town and dropped us off at the next barangay. We were exuberant that time as we were spared from our usual routine of walking back and forth to school.

It was around five o'clock Tuesday afternoon as the sun slowly bid its farewell hinting the arrival of darkness. On my way home, I could already hear the relaxing rhythm made by the insects and the crickets while walking along the mahogany trees towards our house. From afar, I could see the reflection of my mother in the kitchen because of the lamp's flame. As I went closer, I could smell the sweet aroma of sautéed onions and garlic. My stomach got excited as it was clamoring for something delicious. It was Tuesday and market day. For sure, there must be a delicious dish different from the rest of the days that would be served at our table. I was in my fourth grade at that time.

When I went inside our *kubo*, I was greeted by my mother's comforting smile as she transferred her *humba* to a bowl. The steaming dish made my mouth water. It was our signature dish every Tuesday evening since she used to sell chicken parts and other vegetables from our small farm. The money earned would then be bought for a kilo of pork. Minutes later, we started eating our dinner on our medium-sized rectangular table with the lamp at the center. Our surroundings were filled with total darkness except for the glow of fireflies outside, and the light from the moon, and the twinkles of the stars in the night sky.

As we enjoyed eating, my mother spoke something sincere and serious judging from the tone of her voice. Something that I will remember forever. *"Kon moeskuwela mo ug maningkamot, makakaon mo labaw pa ani ug mas haruhay inyong kinabuhi ug ang inyong pamilya. Dili rason ang kawad-on sa kuwarta para dili makab-ot ang inyong mga pangandoy."* (If you study and persevere, you will be able to eat more delicious food than this, and you and your family will live more comfortably.) I was struck by her words of wisdom. I didn't fully understand the deep meaning behind them at that time. Only as I grew older that I slowly realized the true meaning of her words.

We used to sleep as early as eight o'clock at night as the supply of kerosene was limited and budgeted. Unless there was a full moon, we would stay outside our *kubo* and sit on the bamboo bench. I would rest my head on my mother's lap as her hand would caress and stroke my hair looking for some lice. We would look up the stars forming different constellations. It was the Rosary, the Pleiades star cluster, that we always found. She used to tell us her inspiring stories about how obedient she was to her parents. Until we fell asleep and woke up in our woven mat the next morning.

The importance of education was emphasized to me by my mother as she wasn't able to finish her own studies. She worked as a housemaid for her siblings to be able to finish high school. She was an attractive woman as she won the heart of my father who was a nephew of the town's mayor and belonged to one of the prominent families in our town. She used to tell us that we should always dream big, unlike her who had nothing in life. She never believed in herself.

I had the simplest dream before—to work in Shinsaku's Pharmacy (our town's popular pharmacy) after graduating high school. I was a rotten kid. I used to get into fist fights with my classmates, and sometimes I cut classes. No wonder, it was rare for me to get a line of nine during those years. My behavior really disappointed my mother. Until that particular incident came which would later on change me to become better.

As we went to the hospital, I felt the world sinking beneath my feet. My tears cascaded in an endless river of loneliness and pain as I saw my mother on a wheelchair with her left leg wrapped with bandages due to some wounds and bruises. Beside her was her red basket full of groceries. On top of it was pork meat in a yellow-green plastic bag together with some other condiments and ingredients. I hugged her hoping to make her feel safe. I thanked God that she was safe as I couldn't muster up the thought of losing another important person in my life after my father died four days after I was born. The incident made me even stronger. I'd always been an optimistic person, and that incident transformed me. I've often been asked how that moment of transformation felt. For me, it was something that happened naturally like the cracking of an egg and the emergence of a chick.

"It takes a village to raise a child," says an African proverb, but it takes a mother's guidance and love for the child to grow with positivity and determination in life. A mother is irreplaceable as she is the person who can love us genuinely. In her special homemade recipe that suits my taste well, it is a blessing to experience her *savory* love. Every Tuesday, I will always remember two things that have made me who I am today—my mother and her *humba*.

32

The Night-Blooming Jasmine

Jewil Anne Tabiolo

Garden

Our house in Basak was razed to the ground by fire back in 2001. I don't remember much of it since I was just three that time. But years later, we transferred to Talisay City, specifically in Carmen Village. My family took it well and didn't have to do many adjustments since the lot was owned by my grandmother, which means that we knew some relatives who lived there, too. My Lola Levy, from my mother's side, made a small garden at one side of our front yard. In my memory, she always had a green thumb—the plants would never wither in her hands. At present, the garden in front of our house looks very hopeful. Perhaps, it is a living gift offered by the universe to us as a compensation for our losses.

It's hard to believe but my Lola has always gained strength from it. It has given her happiness and a reason to wake up. Every month, she would plant new flowers. Back then, there were Santans, Yellow Bells, Gumamelas, and Dama de Noches. Watching them become fully-bloomed flowers was part of my enjoyment when I was still young since my Lola never allowed me to play outside. It was actually fun witnessing their growth especially when I was guessing what flower would blossom in that week.

Each flower grew differently, always showcasing their beauty as if competing with one another. The tiny Santans grew gracefully like the red polka dots we wore on New Year's Eve to give us good luck. Yellow Bells blossomed attractively like a ballerina's dress, only that their yellow, of course. Beside them were the pinkish red Gumamelas which unfurled themselves breathtakingly like mothers giving birth to their child.

Then, there was the Dama de Noche, a thin-shaped flower that only blooms at night. It was as if giving time for others to manifest the beauty they possess. It didn't compete with the others. It was different from the rest of the flowers.

Home

When the sun would peak to its brightest light, I would no longer find anyone inside our house since my mom was at work. My dad was working abroad and my Lola had to go to the market. Before our house was renovated, I remember that there was a rusty old gate beside our kitchen which served as an access point towards the street. There used to be a riser beneath the gate where I would always sit on and wait for my Lola or for my mom to come home. Every day of my life back then, I did that. I had come to know their routines. At a young age, I had learned to understand that my life was a cycle of staying and leaving.

Mirror

I've never known the reason why they were scared of letting me out of the house. But as years went by, I could somehow connect the dots. My Lola, who has babysat me ever since, told me she was a rebel in the family. Her parents wanted her to stop studying. She did what she was told but she never went home again that day. She left and married my Lolo at the age of 18 and started her own family. She was very young that time, reckless and confused of the circumstances which forced her to grow and stand for the decision she had made.

Every day at dawn, she would wake up with sleepy eyes to sell vegetables in the market. While she was busy there, my Lolo would go to his work in a small barber shop. At that time, they already had four children, hoping that those four would be the blooming flowers from the night and dark trails they had passed through. Later on, my Lolo became a driver in a bank and gained enough money to build a *sari-sari* store. They were able to support their family, but the hardships and challenges left a mark on both of my grandparents. There were also marks left on my Lola's feet. They flayed a lot of skin and left scars that reminded her of the determination she had in order to grow the seeds she had sown. She got them from always washing the dirt off her feet after going to the market—an inadvisable practice especially after having a long and tiring day.

Then came my mother's pregnancy at 22 forcing herself to marry my father. My parents only dated for 6 months before marriage. Now I know why both my Lola and my mom would never allow me to go outside. They were scared of what would happen to me. They were afraid that the scars they had gotten before would be passed on to me, their new sprout. They were frightened that what they had walked on in the past would also be the same trail that I would tread on. They saw me as a mirror that reflects the errors from their past. They locked me inside, hiding me from the same ghosts that chased them in their younger years.

Ocean

I must admit I've never truly lived my childhood and I've missed a lot of fun back then. While everyone sailed the ocean of happiness, I was standing by the shore, waiting for the waves to come back, hoping it would come get me. But my family were the strict bay-keepers that time because they never allowed the sand to be carried away by the waves. They locked me in believing that the waves wouldn't get me.

It was impossible to think that way. That life has been the ocean sending us waves, rough or calm. Whatever tools we have to resist it, it will always come off more strongly than what we expect. The ocean will swish and swing us back and forth until it lands us to the right shore.

Night-Blooming Jasmine (Dama de Noche)

Ever since I was locked up in the house, I have grown up to be the indoor type. I've grown up to be the wallflower in my group of friends. I refused every invitation my friends offered me. I wasn't the good old Santan, the Gumamela, or the Sunflower that everyone else was, but instead I was my *own* flower. I've learned to love being a captive of my own home. My life includes reading books, watching every movie one can think of, staring at an endless blank space, or eating a bowl of cereal even if it's already dinner time, and a lot more drudging things one can imagine. But these things make me safe, or at least, my Lola or mom thought so. My routines are like the unfamiliar built-in applications in someone's phone, the ones you never delete because you're afraid it might corrupt the system of your gadget. Or, the old worn-out shoes you keep telling yourself not to use anymore, but you still end up wearing them, anyway.

Those were the pieces that make up my whole being. People may never identify me as the beautiful one, the talented one, or the friendly one. Like all the famous flowers in my Lola's garden, other people are those that bloom at the time everyone expects them to do so. But I am the night-blooming Jasmine. The Dama de Noche that my loved ones have designed me to be. The flower that blooms at its comfort. The flower that blooms differently compared to the rest.

The History of You and Me: Through Reversed Time

Brenzy Kaye Maquilan

December 2017

I could clearly remember how it felt like when I was a melting ice cube subjected to heat in my seat and in a large crowd. I wasn't going to perform and it wasn't some kind of stage fright. It was just an overwhelming feeling when my insides felt like the petals of a dandelion blown away, dancing through the thin air. If you ask what blew me away, well, it was a pair of brown eyes, a beautiful voice, and a beating heart of the person standing in front of me, in front of a large crowd. I was an ice cube being subjected to the heat of his eyes radiating through every single glance, of his voice singing the sweetest words, and of his beating heart that I always longed to hear. I couldn't forget how his eyes searched for me through the crowd, filtering faces after faces until his eyes glimmered like a diamond when he had set and locked his gaze on me as he sang the line "Darling, you look perfect tonight..." while gesturing towards my direction. The crowd cheered and suddenly I was the only rose in a field of sunflowers. It wasn't the cheer of the crowd or the line from the song that sent my heart fluttering like bird's wings. It was how I found home in a pair of brown eyes and a heartbeat.

October 2017

At around dinner time, I walked away from the group. I walked alone feeling the cold breeze of what I thought was coming from the mountain, still hearing faint laughter and cheers from where I just came from. Amidst the faint laughter and cheers there was a deafening silence everywhere as the sad hues of blue have taken over the skies, but I felt no fear walking alone as I searched for him, as I searched for my peace. I slowly breathed in the air of loneliness and tasted the taste of freedom in every breeze as I stopped and stood by the pool while looking at the magnificent sight of the city lights reaching out to the stars in the sky.

I have always loved looking at the city lights and the night sky. It makes me understand what little things that come together can do. When you look at it from afar, they're all just little lights. But when they come along with different brightness and colors, they become a masterpiece. Looking at these views always gets me lost in thoughts and just then, I was about to get even more lost than ever.

I looked down from where I was standing and there, I saw the perfect addition to the masterpiece that I was just beholding. And yet again, I was getting even more lost in the moment. There he was sitting at the cliff side, staring at the same view I was getting lost into. The deafening silence was replaced with the gentle hum of the cold night. The loneliness in the air became a rope pulling me towards him.

I couldn't help but adore how perfect the scenery was! How he was peacefully sitting there. How two of the things I love came together to form one perfect composition in one perfect moment. And so, I allowed myself to be drawn to him. I sat on the patch of grass beside him as he looked at me. Just then my heart skipped a beat as I saw his eyes twinkle like the stars. We sat there in silence and right then, I knew he was the one I'd always wanted to share that breathtaking sight with.

March 2017

The music was roaring and the lights were wild. We attended our friend's debut in a small resort near my house and it was around 9:00 in the evening when we decided to go home. The party went on and the rest of the group was still dancing to the loud music as we waited outside the resort for a tricycle, but nothing came since it was already quite late. We stood under the lonely lamp post by the road with our bags in hand. The night was quiet except for the sound of the crickets and the waves of the ocean nearby whispering everyone to sleep. We've been waiting a bit too long that we decided to just start walking home instead.

The streets were empty. Everyone was asleep and not a single vehicle passed by. I knew I had to be scared with the thought of walking in the dark in an unfamiliar place, but I wasn't. He was there with me and I knew everything would just be fine. Instead of walking in silence and in fear, we ran and walked and talked like we owned the place. We stood in the middle of the road and just laughed to our hearts' content, and then we danced to the music of our synchronized heartbeats. That moment made us feel so young, in love, and carefree. Nobody was there to stop us and not a single eye would judge us.

I remembered years ago, I'd always dreamed of a guy walking me home, but I knew that was impossible because my house was too far from the jeepney stop that I still needed to get another ride just to reach our house. But there he was walking me home late that night on a deserted street. Who would've thought my daydreams would unintentionally come to life? Who would've thought he would be that guy to walk me home?

June 2016

When the school year started, I was determined to be a lowkey student to save myself from another potential drama from this senior high. The first day of class turned out to be like an abstract painting—different people from different schools and places. A chaotic mix! It wasn't like any other school year I had before when new faces became less and less each year. I was always surrounded with familiar faces back then, but I never really had any true friends. Because of that I was completely thrilled to meet new faces which happened to be the majority of the class.

The second day was pretty much different. There were more activities and most of them were group activities. There was this one activity where we were randomly grouped. I awkwardly joined my assigned group which was mostly composed of girls and only one boy. I tried to be quiet in order to avoid so much attention as we brainstormed how we would creatively present the school rule on tardiness assigned to us. We ended up with a role-play where a love team was needed to spice up the presentation. For some reason, I was chosen to be paired up with the only guy in the group. After all the planning, we had a bit of time left to get to know the other members. We introduced ourselves to the group and that was how I knew Lance Catadman.

In the role play, I played as Lance's crush and he would be acting as if he was running late for class and would rush through the school gates where we would bump into each other, and from then on, I would be helping him become more punctual for I was a "model student."

The acting began and we stood in our places. Lance was on the left side of the room and I was in front of him. Our groupmates acting as guards were standing by the door and the other students were scattered in other areas. I walked in first and Lance was behind me. I was rummaging through my bag as if I was searching for something. Then he tried to get ahead of me in a hurry and ended up bumping into me. He looked back to say sorry and was surprised to see me, his crush.

His eyes met mine and that was when I suddenly zoned into the moment. Everyone else slowed down. My vision focused on him and him alone blurring the rest of the surroundings, and the only thing I could clearly hear was the sound of my heartbeat. His gaze drove me to the farthest end of the infinite galaxy and his eyes were a pool of intense sincerity. I snapped back to reality when the crowd teased us and said that we're the first love team of the school year.

Yes, it was slow motion. No, it wasn't part of the role play. Yes, it was like a scene from the movie which I never expected could happen in reality. I didn't want to make a big deal out of it, but little did I know that it was how our story would begin.

Balay-Laaganan

Shyamelissa Sunder

I do *not* love going out of my house.

"*Laag*" and "*walwal*" are two mostly used Cebuano terms that denote going out to socialize. I'm not really a big "socializer." Since I was in junior high, a lot of my friends and acquaintances have invited me to go to some malls after class or on holidays to have fun. I suppose I have declined quite a lot of them in the past few years for many reasons. Some of them were true, some of them were half-truths. But let's not dig into that. They just learned to stop asking me to come with them because it's just as exhausting as trying to force a toddler to eat her vegetables.

Balay

My house is in Minglanilla, Cebu. It's quite far from the city, a 30-minute public transport ride if it's a good day, and a full-blown hour if the traffic despises you.

No, my house doesn't have the stereotypical picket-white fence, but it does have a broken-down Nissan March that is probably as old as me, rotting in the front yard. It's in a low-cost housing subdivision of row houses, so our house doesn't really stand out. It has the same faded yellow paint on the outside with a brick-colored roof as every other house does. What makes my house different from the rest is the strikingly obvious uncut lawn. The greens are slowly swallowing up our yard on the side. I wouldn't be surprised if it would colonize our Nissan sooner or later. You see, we can't afford a landscaper and none of us have the time to do gardening work because all of my siblings are busy. That includes me, too.

The house is situated perfectly on the corner of the subdivision, by a wall that leads to a ravine. Both my older sisters hate the fact that we live right beside that ravine, but I think it's a good thing. The trees from it give our house shade and help cool the temperature around us during sunny days. It is also aesthetically pleasing to look at, especially on rainy days. The trees would dance under the rain, with the wind as its partner. It reminds me of the filming location of young-adult movies set in the Pacific North-West like *Twilight*.

Inside our house are blue walls that remind me of the sea on a surfing day. I can only imagine the moment a wave curls and hits by sunlight—that's the perfect shade of blue on our walls. Our house has everything a person living in this century needs. A good supply of water and electricity, cable television, a good couch and a charging station right beside it, a bedroom with the most comfortable queen-sized bed that I love to roll around on to add five more minutes to my sleep. (Don't ask me why I'm late to school sometimes.) My family has two adorable dogs—a medium-sized one and a palm-sized one, both are extremely furry. And most importantly, our portal to the world, a good WIFI connection, though I won't personally say it's good enough.

When Mom's Home

My mom is one of the modern heroes of the country. She is an overseas Filipino worker. She was one of the Filipinos who got enticed with working abroad, as its hype back in the '80s was at its peak. She got to work in Oman first and now, she's in Kuwait. Both countries are in the Middle East or as she calls it, *"lugar nga pulos ba's"* (a place filled with sand). Back then, she'd only come home every two years, but as she climbed up the corporate ladder at work in one of the major retailers in Kuwait, she now gets to come home every year for a month.

When my mom is home, she'd always smell of Kuwait. I'd describe that smell as a mix of her favorite laundry detergent and the smell of well-kept clothes in a closet, with a hint of department-store smell, of new clothes and stock room spaces, and traces of airport smell, a mix of luggage-smell and paper-smell. Even the boxes she brings and the LBC *balikbayan* box would exactly smell like that when we open them.

When she's home and has already recuperated from her long flight, she'd do two of her most favorite things—doing laundry and cleaning the house. I remember one time when I was peacefully taking a nap on our couch while my mom was doing laundry and the distinct smell of my mother's laundry woke me up. A mixture of Ariel and Downy, her favorite laundry detergent and fabric conditioner. I felt my mom approach me on the spot where I was having my peaceful slumber. I heard her telling me to get up because she needed someone to hang the clothes she so passionately washed. I remember responding with a strained groan. I believe it may be the sound of an animal from the Animal Planet TV show I watched earlier that day. I heard my mom chuckle from a distance as I chose to continue sleeping. The whirring of the washing machine managed to lull me to sleep again, but my mom would not have it. She nudged my shoulder forcing me to open my eyes and see the blaring light from the outside of our window. I made the face I always make every time I come across a vehicle with its head lamps in high beams. Like when I go home from school and wait for a jeepney on the sidewalks of Basak.

I sat up groggily, reminded of my sister who woke up drunk from the night before when she decided to finish off the bottle of Cabernet we had from our New Year's celebration. I took the pail full of clean clothes and asked my mom, *"Nganong ako man?"* (Why me?) and she just simply answered, *"Ang-ang mas maayo man ka manghayhay kaysa mamilo"* (Because you are better at hanging clothes than folding them). That "roast" was so harsh for me that I actually considered going back to sleep after doing her bidding. Thanks, Mom.

When my mom is home, she'd clean up the house. Not just arrange-it-here-and-there cleaning, but it's the I-don't-want-anymore-dirt-on-this-house-ever-again fashion. When she's done, the entire house would exactly smell like her. Our house would smell like a little Kuwait in the Philippines.

When Mom is home, she would cook food, real food—a variety of them like vegetables, pork, and my personal favorite, the *utan-kamunggay*. The aroma of the spices from the soup would engulf the house as if a tear gas was thrown into the house, you can almost taste the soup itself. My mom doesn't allow instant noodles, canned goods, and other ready-to-cook foods for us. Our dining table would be full of fruits like those during traditional Filipino celebration of New Year's where the table is laden with 13 round fruits.

See? Why should I go out if our house has restaurant-like food and fruits, right?

Sa Balay ra ko Molaag (I'll Just Enjoy at Home)

My not liking to go out much says a lot about me as a person. First, I am lazy. I don't like going through the entire process of getting ready and choosing what to wear. I don't like walking for three minutes from our house to our subdivision gates. I despise public transport because I'm not a fan of people getting into my personal space. Going out and the process of it are just too much for me. Second, I don't like spending money just for the sake of it. Why should I spend money on restaurants for food that can be cooked at home? Why should I buy something unnecessary as new clothes when I still have a lot of clothes in my closet? Why should I spend on public transport when I can just stay at home and have all the space for myself, not even breaking a sweat? Exactly! Third, I am uncomfortable when I'm out of my comfort zone, especially when it's unexpected. Yet, it's true that I wish to change because deep inside me I want to take some risks. For in doing so, I will find adventures in life. I don't want to be stagnant in one place and lead a life of robotic existence. Finally, for me, the most important event in the house is when my mom is around. Even if she roasts me for the fun of it. Even if I get an earful of her nagging every time I don't do my chores. When my mom is here, our house would feel more of a home.

Ignacio

Samantha Tabotabo

Salutations

I enjoy rain. There is a sense of relief and serenity that washes over me whenever it rains, especially when I hear the pitter-patter against the roof or the windows. What else can I say? I am a rain person, a pluviophile.

Rain can bring back a lot of precious memories. Like that particular moment I was listening to *the bootleg boy*'s playlist one wet afternoon. I was closing my eyes as each song mixed with the soothing rhythm of the rain from the outside. While I was in the middle of drinking my coffee, all of a sudden I heard a sound that disturbed me. I looked down at the window and saw a kitten caterwauling, stuck in a cavernous drainage. It came to my attention that the water in the drainage was slowly rising up. I had to do something. I couldn't just leave the kitten out there and die, and let my conscience haunt me forever. So I rushed down, took a dustpan, went to the drainage near our house, dipped down, and carefully let the kitten in. She was all covered in mud and was shivering so much that I had to send the poor thing to the bathroom and give her a warm bath. Her fur was as white as snow and her eyes as blue as sapphire. An angel!

As soon as she was all dried up, I fed her and tucked her in a light blue shirt I found in the cabinet and then both of us fell asleep. When I woke up, I found her lying next to my shoulder. It was at that moment that I decided to keep her. By the time her sapphire eyes opened, she never stopped meowing at me. She started following me wherever I went. Her greeting warmed my heart. An act of gratitude, a warm greeting you might say, an embracing fancy way of saying hello, a salutation. It was during that moment, that I felt something, something I hadn't felt for a long time ago.

In a Name

A fire had awoken my dying heart. That's what it felt like. Since then, I knew that inside me, deep down, lies a girl sinking into a pit of nothingness. One might say I'm living a fake life. Correct. When you're having this little fake life it's as if it almost completely takes over that you can't even get those little glimpses of the truth anymore. I was lost and this mask was starting to eat me up, and I was becoming this person I didn't know. When someone is going through that, they're not them anymore. They lose that spark. Things like that don't go away; they only escalate.

But ever since the cat came into my life, something felt different—something good. It felt like seeing a friend you hadn't seen for a long time and as soon as I opened my eyes and saw her lying beside me, my heart felt like warm butter sliding down on a hot toast. I was genuinely happy. It gave me the idea to give her a name. A name that would signify her mere existence. And it would be *Ignacio*. In Latin it means fire. Ignacio was my fire—we were each other's fire, for I saved her life and she saved mine.

Fire's Gone

It was like any other day. The usual cold embrace of the sun's breath awoke me from my slumber. Roosters sang signifying that the night before had bled today. Sunrays illuminated my entire room as a bit of their brightness blinded my eyes. It was like any other day, or so I thought. There was an awfully strange energy hanging on my back. "*Asa diay si Ignacio?*" (Where is Ignacio?) I asked myself. I didn't worry about her absence at first. I thought she was in the kitchen feasting on her cat food. As I went down, people greeted me with a peculiar look on their faces. The atmosphere was like a ghost town. Confusion entered my body with his *compadre*, Anxiety.

Anxiety then came running towards me to grab my throat—to grab the words that were supposed to be used in asking what had happened. I heard a loud sniff from the outside. As I went out, I saw my brother looking down at Ignacio, lying on the ground, lifeless. I ran towards my breathless little feline. She was as hard as stone and I noticed her collar was gone. I couldn't bear the pain. It felt like I was shot directly at my heart a hundred times. I rushed to my room, drowning myself in my own tears.

After an hour and a half, I had finally mustered up the courage to ask what caused her death. She was tortured, locked up in a jar, and was shaken. She was used as a "catching ball" by our neighbors' child. Anger consumed me. I took a glimpse from my window and landed at the sight of our neighbors' evil offspring. All hell broke loose when my eyes landed on her wrist. The collar I gave to my beloved Ignacio was on her filthy wrist. I wanted to barge into their house and declare "This is Sparta!" on the kid but I was stopped by my grandmother. *"Bata pa man god"* (She's still a child) was the line that struck me most. How could someone dismiss such vicious action with no punishment?

Disgusted, hurt, and petrified. Three words that perfectly described how I felt towards the kid. I was angry and terrified at the same time. A child was able to claim an innocent life. A child! She gave me the impression that she never felt guilty, not even a tad remorse shown on her face. It was as if nothing ever happened. Each time I looked at the child's face just reminded me of what she'd done, and it stung as if a part of me, something happy was ripped from my chest. And I couldn't stop the bleeding. Losing Ignacio felt as if the sun bid its final farewell.

Discernments

Malls—the other place where I like to contemplate on the things happening in my life. It was on a sunny afternoon when I decided to go walk around the corners of SM City Cebu. It's always during the weekdays I find it comforting to be in malls simply because it isn't that crowded. While I was passing by different shops, I stumbled upon a familiar place that I used to go to when I was a child—a playroom. As I leaned towards the glass I saw kids playing around like there's no tomorrow. How I wished I could go back to that phase! When all you ever worry about was only your mother scolding you because you'd already used up so many *sandos* (undershirts) for playing *dakop-dakop* (tags).

My eyes landed on two children who were creating a commotion at the playroom. One little girl cried so loudly pointing towards the little boy who was holding a vehicle toy. Every time the little girl tried to go towards him, he stayed a distance and covered his toy. The little girl's face turned bloody red as her tears turned into an ocean while the boy just remained calm. The look that the little boy gave was surprisingly similar to the child who took the life of Ignacio. I sat down at a café and asked myself again, "Why did she have to kill Ignacio?" After a long silence, I had a realization.

A child may behave viciously at times, I get it. It may simply signify that a child is longing for attention, or there's something that he or she wants to get hold of. However, children who are cruel to animals are a different story. I've had some help from my arguably reliable confidante, the Internet. To summarize everything I've gathered, children who are abusive to animals may end up being a sociopath. Because of my burning wrath towards the child, I had a hard time deciding what's right or not. I was toying my mind with the idea that she would turn out to be a sociopath someday. Suddenly, I heard a strange voice on the other side of my brain. "Maybe the child does not understand the concept of death, that she is simply too young to discern how her actions could take the life of another. All of that was beyond her understanding."

December 26, 2017

The sun had set and dusk had prevailed. I felt the warm embrace of the city lights and the cold mist. As I wore the smile that I knew wasn't genuine, I felt like screaming on the inside. I felt like I was crawling back down towards my pit of nothingness again. I never felt so empty, like there was a huge void in my soul. I knew I had friends, but I still felt so lonely. Ignacio had been the only one I could run to. Although she didn't actually talk, she gave me comfort. I could ramble on about what's going on in my life right now, but I'm scared of becoming someone's burden when they could have a million things going on in their lives as well that are much worse than mine. I can just break down in tears when the load I'm carrying becomes too heavy. But every time this happens, I just remind myself to keep going. For myself. For my friend, Ignacio.

Lucid Dreams

Blue Rain

Lance Roi Catadman

Rain

When I was a kid, I always loved the rain. Maybe because I was taught that rain would give life to plants, animals, and all life on Earth. When Mama Marj allowed me to play under the rain, I would jump up and down in delight on our small mattress as I stripped off my shirt and shorts, leaving my underwear exposed for everyone to see. I was just young then so I felt no shame. I would rush outside our gate with my eyes closed, greeted by raindrops that pelted my young, tender skin. I would scream out loud in joy, unaware of how annoying my trembling voice was. Then again, I was just young. I didn't mind at all. I was just living like how every other organism on Earth would under this majestic rain. I then understood why rain gave life to everything. It wasn't an amazing scientific discovery that would blow minds across the entire world. Rather, it was a life lesson that I've been cherishing all these years.

We lived in a small village in Punta Princesa. Back then, it was a small and peaceful community. Our neighbors knew each other well and were very friendly towards each other. It had just the right number of trees to provide all of us fresh air. No wonder they chose to live in that village. I remember having a group of friends who, although were much older, played with me as if I was one of them. Unfortunately, I can't remember their names simply because I was just five years old back then. But I do remember having a *kuya* figure from one of them. His name was Lyle. I didn't call him *Kuya* like every other kid would when they meet a man older than them. I just called him merely by his name.

Lyle was the jolliest among my long-forgotten group of friends. He would actually be the one to start the games when all of us gathered in front of their red gate. That one game I always liked was "*tsinelasay*." It is a game of striking one slipper with its pair until it crosses the chalk-drawn finish line. I remember being very good at it despite my young age. It was partly the reason why I liked it. The other reason would be that I just wanted to show off my favorite Spider-Man slippers. I remember Lyle having handsome features like a big pair of eyes, a pointed nose, and fair white skin. At least that was what Mama Marj said were "handsome" features. The mentality of Western features being the exemplar of "beautiful" and "handsome" was still very common back then. I also remember Lyle having a sister who actually played with me oftentimes when he was not around because of homework.

One day, when I was outside bathing in the rain while jumping around puddles, I heard Lyle doing his signature scream as he rushed out of his house. We tried playing *tsinelasay* but failed really hard because the wet ground and the broken asphalt complemented well to hinder our slippers from even moving an inch. Instead, we played *bahaw-bahaw*, which was my all-time despised game because I had dwarf legs. There was never a single *bahaw-bahaw* game where I was not held captive. After all the fun, I heard a loud angry female voice from Lyle's house that said, "Lyle! *Pauli na kay masakit na sad ka!*" (Lyle! Come home now or you'll get sick!) I felt absolutely confused when his mother scolded him. I knew that long periods under the rain could give someone colds or fever. Even my mother would be worried about me when I play. But Lyle's mother was different. There was definitely something odd about the way she yelled at him. It wasn't a scold of concern. It was a scream of anger. She yelled at him like every mother would when they got disappointed of their child. What he could have possibly done that day, I never knew. All I understood was that the rain wasn't just a symbol of life and joy. I realized that it was also a home to different stories, be it happy or sad. A piece of reality started unfolding upon me, like rain with a sudden strike of lightning and thunder.

Blue

Wednesday, September 21, 2017. It was the third day of our 33rd Intramurals and University Days at the University of San Jose-Recoletos. The Forward Publications of the College Department and The Josenian Premier of the Senior High School Department collaborated for the first time to cover the different events of the Intramurals. I was assigned to cover the basketball and table tennis events, together with Jara and Mon. It was late in the afternoon when rain started to pour on the metropolis. Though feeling disappointed since many sports events were stopped, I savored the little droplets that fell on my forehead, and smiled. Ever since, I have loved the rain. I loved how the drizzles sparkled when car headlights beamed through them. I loved how they trickled down from tree leaves to fall on the ground. I loved how it called me to bathe myself, to cleanse from all the negativity that had happened ever since. Everything about it was just lovely and so magical.

After the rain poured, everyone, or at least half from each publication, gathered in the Forward Publications' office for shelter. I was helping Mon because he wasn't able to get the results for the men's division of table tennis. Jara was already anxious because of the weather condition. I could tell she didn't like the rain, or maybe I just loved it that much that I assumed other people hated it. Anyway, Jara tried to convince those who lived in Southern Cebu to go with her, but to no avail. Marianne, a close friend of ours, was still busy helping out with Forward. Mon, on the other hand, was still waiting for his final event for the day. Aside from covering the table tennis events, Mon was also a player of the sport. I watched him play in the morning on that day and found myself amazed by his superb footwork and reaction time. That left me the only one available to accompany Jara. I was already planning on going home after the rain stopped. So, it wasn't much of a problem at all.

I said goodbye to all the staff in the office as I grabbed my laptop bag and my red and gray knapsack. Outside the office, Jara and I prepared our umbrellas, ready to set foot on the flooded streets of Colon. Little did we know that by the time we got out of the campus, it would become an honest struggle. The gradual rise of water from the drainage canals was quite noticeable. Every jeepney that passed by was fully occupied. The rain got stronger and stronger, and thunderclaps started to echo along the streets.

Jara and I walked by the flooded hallway of the university. Our socks were all soaking wet but we had no choice. Eventually, there were vacant jeepneys but they were not operating. Some were operating but they didn't accept passengers. Luckily, a vacant 09G jeepney passed by and we rode on it without any hesitation. I gestured to let Jara in first. As we closed our umbrellas, the rain drenched through our clothes aggressively, thus making them wet and heavy. As we rode on the jeepney, the driver all of a sudden said that he would still be taking some rest before he could accept more passengers. Jara was utterly disappointed while I was feeling downcast, like the gray sky that was blue just that morning. The jeepney then stopped by a building near the Magellan's Cross where we decided to get off. The floodwater in the area was already above ankle level. I watched in awe as the water near my feet rose and tried to pull me towards it. Jara then snapped me out of my trance and suggested that she call her dad to pick her up. The only problem was that only she would get to ride since her dad was driving a motorcycle. I then reassured her that I'd be fine and that I'd be able to go home on my own. Suddenly, the previous driver who dropped us by the building called us and said that he was done taking rest and was now ready to accept passengers. We were enormously lucky.

The jeepney was slowly occupied by different people with different encounters with the rain. One carried a child with her, one brought her produce to sell, and one wore a fine dress but got drenched and dirty. Everyone was chattering mindlessly that their voices were stronger than the sound of rain. I didn't mind at all. But one thing I observed among the passengers was that they were all smiling. They weren't mad that it rained. They were just happy to be interacting with others inside the jeepney and sharing their experiences. Jara also joined in with the interaction and enjoyed talking with the strangers. I, on the other hand, just enjoyed observing the positivity they all displayed. Later, everyone turned quiet and the sound of the rain, cars, and water current were the only things that could be heard of. Almost everyone, including Jara, fell asleep. They must have felt tired trying to save themselves from the rain and find either a shelter or a jeepney.

By the time I arrived at the gas station in Summit, I bid farewell to Jara since she just lived in

Pardo. Though it was raining hard, I still stood in line in the usual queue I take during regular class days. Together with five people, we each used umbrellas for protection. The strangers were a couple, two workers, and a student. I knew each of us had a different story to tell about the rain and what we'd been through. Eventually, I found myself spacing out once more, staring at the rain for a good three minutes. I then realized the piece of reality that unfolded upon me many years ago.

I examined almost every drop and realized that they all looked the same but were different in a way. Some fell fast and the others quite slow. Some were big and some were small. Some fell on trees and the others on automobiles. I realized that we were no different from these raindrops. We live life differently to some extent, yet we end up with the same conclusion and that is falling to the ground. I realized that we are all in one with the rain. We are all droplets of different stories. Each of us gives meaning to this life we have, just like how the rain gives life to everything on Earth. And as I reached home, I brought with me this piece of reality and cherished the day the blue rain poured down upon me.

March 4, 2018
original

Passionately Drunk on Writing

Devey Joy Gaviola

According to Ray Bradbury, "You must stay drunk on writing so reality cannot destroy you." I stared blankly at the white screen of an empty document trying to figure out how I wanted my words to dance. I must say that if writing were a drink, I could have been alcoholic even before I entered the adolescence stage. However, like any other drink, there is this kind of liquor I wanted to avoid. This honestly might give me a failing grade, but I am not really fond of writing memoirs. If I were to choose between writing fiction and nonfiction, I would choose the former in a heartbeat. As a matter of fact, this was a puzzle I needed to answer. Giving up momentarily, I decided to open up the notebook that contained the skeletons of my life—the skeletons I had buried in the deepest part of graves, on the floors of Marianas Trench, and in the core of my heart.

Just by flipping the cover page, I could smell the rotting memories of my childhood, the putrid stench of loneliness and the mixed whiff of hope and anger. Its uneven pages tattered on the edges, the leaves holding on to the tiny threads binding them from the spine as if it were their lifelines. But almost a decade ago, it was a sleek journal with a front cover of a children's movie about some singing high school teens. On December 22, 2008, I wrote my first entry in my first-ever diary. The first ten pages of it were about the days of playing with friends and watching movies. Its innocence and pure bliss almost colored the writings with bright hues only to appear to be endless scribbles of heartaches, pain, and suffering penned in ink and tears. It was the time when writing became the only thing that kept my childhood-self sane. I wrote in tight knuckles and stifled sobs. I wanted the world to know how everything—the bullying, the verbal abuse, and the desolation were too much to bear, yet I also did not want to. Whichever it might be, I scribbled them down. The entries were a combination of Kurt Vonnegut's *Universal Shape of Stories—Boy Meets Girl* and *From Bad to Worse*, only that I did not get back what I lost. This mood continued on to the next notebooks I kept.

It was only when I reached fourth grade that I discovered that writing was not limited to diaries. My first story was a fanfiction of my favorite anime shows. I was in my bed, envisioning myself walking towards two portals. I needed to decide whether I would enter the world of a card captor in a red dress and a star baton or in a universe where *shuriken* and *jutsu* existed. I told my brother of this "vision" the next day. His half-hearted attention drove me to write this vision instead. More fanfiction stories were created until I decided to draft an original story. My first readers, who were my friends, commended my amateur works.

It was the only time in my grade school life when I felt genuinely happy. Finally, somebody recognized my imagination and ideas. At this moment, I knew that I wanted to become a writer. I did not care whether I would become famous or not. I just needed an outlet to distract myself from the reality that continued stabbing and ignoring my silent prayers of "I hope I will be happy someday."

My brother and I had a huge fight that ended up with him tearing half of the pages of my diary and screaming how worthless it was. I was never a crybaby in front of my family, but my tears were non-stop as I picked up my dearest notebook of what was left of it. With clammy hands, I tried to tape the pieces back like how I had always kept stitching my ruptured will of living. My classmates made fun of my stories. My relatives told me I would not have a future with this "simple" hobby I wanted to pursue. It was then when I realized that being a writer was not an easy task. Making the words dance to your desired beat was not enough. No matter how I would get drunk with writing, the reality would slap me back the next day like a head-pounding hangover.

In my seventh grade, we were required to write diaries about our daily school activities and events. We were to submit every Friday, and our adviser would return it on the following Monday. On June 13, 2012, I wrote about how nervous I was to walk in a school foreign to me, and how terrified I was of what future emotional beatings I would meet. It happened that our class adviser was our English teacher, too. He was an openly gay person with a mood that would never drop. His eyes lit up with much gusto whenever he would discuss Philippine literature. I will never forget what he wrote in my diary on June 16, 2012: "I had fun reading your diary. It was informative and detailed. I also marveled at your writing prowess." These three sentences and less than twenty words ignited my dying dream. He soon recommended that I join the school's publication, which I happily obliged. In my last year in junior high, I ended up as the English Editor. It was one of the greatest achievements I have gained in my entire writing journey.

My inner turmoil did not end in grade school. It seemed like I was a magnet for bullying and verbal abuse. I was again criticized for my "different looks"—either because of my big brown eyes, gapped front teeth, nerdy aura, or simply because I was not as beautiful as my best friends, which they found really rather odd. Time and time again, I would get drunk on writing with a desperate wish of forgetting the reality. I confined myself to the worlds of Suzanne Collins, Charlotte Brontë, Jane Austen, and different Wattpad writers. My self-confidence was on the floor and I would find myself writing in mixed tears and ink. I could have penned more than a hundred pages about it and then no more. No, I was not tired of writing. I was tired of writing the same old feelings. Like crying about something, writing over and over again about similar stuff would exhaust a person, too, until he or she would no longer do it.

Eureka! I exhaled in relief as I closed the pages of the violet notebook where I last wrote my sentiments. It was a Christmas gift, like my first diary from my best friend who adored my stories. Nonfiction's strong flavor of factual information, hint of reminiscence, and taste of subtle creativity were too much even for an "alcoholic" like me. It burned my throat, flamed my tongue, and soured my face. It mirrored how I felt about the real world and how I hated the need to get back to the past I had tried so hard to forget. Why would someone start digging back their rotten skeletons?

In the first entry of my personal blog, I wrote about forgiveness and happiness. I must have drunk a cocktail for the lightness of my subject. Perhaps, I needed the time to recollect the past no matter how painful it was. Some wounds needed opening for sterilization and better healing. My avoidance of nonfiction could have suppressed my ability to write, to guide the dance of words. I even did not participate in any kind of writing opportunities when I entered senior high. Aside from the busy schedule, my depression blew my interest in it.

I sat again in front of my laptop, attempting to choreograph the next dance of words. I was determined to change. "Devey, I have always found that each step we take in life is to be regretted once we begin to wonder how many steps might have been possible." These were the last words my seventh-grade adviser wrote in my diary. However, I was determined not to walk on the same path anymore. I made a set of resolutions of trying new liquors, writing different genres of literature. The next time I would write, it would not only mirror my sentiments but of people. It would not be my truth, but the truth that everyone should know. Someday, I would pen a book that would create happiness and ignite inspiration in others. I wanted to take away the loneliness of the people that once mirrored mine.

I knew it would not be easy. It was and would never be. More criticism and rejections would come in my way. I may or may not succeed. The reality would continue to be itself as I would try to continually get drunk on writing. If this became my lifelong vice, then I would taste all kinds of liquor no matter how sweet or bitter they are. I would let their addictive flavor seep into my throat until I create the greatest dance of words, and the fulfillment of this dream started when I typed the first words of this paper and drank the hated liquor of nonfiction.

~~Confined~~

Jeanne Ross Heredia

The hospital has given me so much trauma for the past few years. Well, I've developed such trauma and it just so happened that it was during my stay in that place. That trauma started when my Mama had a series of heart attacks and we had to come back and forth to the hospital for almost half a year. I've witnessed people pass away several times that I grew accustomed to it. But this one incident has developed an additional fear to my trauma box. It was that day when Mama had another attack and it was I who witnessed it first. I was so preoccupied and worried at the same time that my thoughts did not stop running. I was just sitting outside the Emergency Room cubicles when a corpse was carried out. It was a sudden shock to my brain. "I am in front of a corpse" was the only thing that covered up all my flooded thoughts. But that was not the only thing that bothered me the most. The corpse was then situated at the back of the cubicle where four patients were being attended to. She was covered by detachable whiteboards just so it wouldn't bother passersby. But it did bother me.

We are all bound to die.

And so when it was my turn to slice the cake, I felt afraid. I felt the fear even with the knowledge that my sickness was not that deadly. But I guess it was not the disease that scared me. It was the thought of me dying inside a four-walled room without anyone to hold on to.

Being hospitalized means turning ourselves into a human pin cushion. But I am a special pin cushion; we (my family) are. We have really thin veins that only 10% (approximately) of the medical technologist population can draw our blood in just one insertion which means a lot of "swimming" underneath my skin happens. I was brought to the hospital in the second week of my recurring fever. It was overwhelming because (1) I was going to break the family record that we only get hospitalized if someone's giving birth, (2) needles, and (3) more needles. I was not admitted immediately on my arrival. The nurse suggested that I get one last blood test and come back the next day. She said I might be okay tomorrow which was exactly the opposite of what happened when I had my blood drawn in their laboratory. I almost fainted because I was poked (with the needle) ten times or more and I already felt dizzy. Good thing Ate Ikit and her husband were already there. Ate Ikit is my older sister Ann's best friend and is currently a pediatrician and a professor. They studied Medical Technology together. It was Ate Ikit's husband who noticed me almost fainting because I was all pale and wobbly. I was then rushed to the E.R. just to receive a bigger poke of needle on my hand for the I.V.

It wasn't a bad idea at all, being hospitalized. I had a new soft pillow and I was able to rest from tons of school work and social pressure. Well, that's what I thought. I could finally testify on "Rest is for the weak." I had to answer so many interview questions about my health history and entertain more nurses and doctors every hour. Quite a hassle, but that was not my main problem. Surely, four days could be considered short. But not when you stayed in a room and slept all day 24/7. I had to stay in my room alone most of the time during those four days because everybody else had to work. It was lonely, I couldn't even eat because my stomach did not welcome food at all, and my gut hurt so bad for some reason. My escape from all of these was only sleeping with my pillow tightly attached to my painful gut.

The loneliest thing that might happen to you when you are being hospitalized is celebrating your birthday in your room. Not being able to eat chocolate cake and ice cream because I couldn't consume dark colored food, and simply not being able to eat because of zero appetite. Even looking at the food on the TV screen made me want to puke. It was miserable hating something that I loved so much. Yes, I had so many visitors that day. My friends came over and made me laugh. My auntie was there in the evening to check on me and everybody brought food (that in the end was still consumed by them alone). My family was there, too. But there was like 3 to 4 hours that they left me alone again so they could buy themselves food, which made me think so much. I was thankful for everyone who made an effort on visiting me and surprising me, but above all the gratefulness was the thought, *"Wow, I just turned 16 inside this confined room!"* And ever since that day, I have considered my birthday an ordinary day.

I was sent home with the doctor's strict order that I should have a complete bed rest for at least 3 days after being discharged from the hospital. I was still suffering from bad motion sickness at that time (since childhood, actually) so I had to go home riding a taxi with open windows. All I had was a pillow in hand. But it felt comforting, having something to hold on to.

Standing up was a bit of a challenge, I was still dizzy. I made my way to the terrace and was welcomed by our dogs and it strangely felt like visiting a new friend's house for the first time. It felt and looked big. I entered the house and went on the couch to remove my shoes, having my head down all the time. And as I looked up, I was astonished by the view that I saw. It was a white wall with black and brown moldings and bricks attached to it. It was an open view to the ceiling, revealing an antique-looking chandelier. The stairs looked perfect with black tiles and black railings. It was as if I was checking out a new place to move in. I felt so overwhelmed that I wanted to puke. So I tried to relax. *Is this the right place? Is it really this big?* I was confused about what my brain was trying to say to me. I was just away for four days, but coming home felt like I went abroad for several years already. I went to my room and felt the same overwhelming sensation. *How can something change so quickly?* I grabbed the pillow and held on it so tightly hoping that all of my thoughts would go away. So I just closed my eyes and called it a day.

I woke up the next day almost suffocating. The first thing I saw was a white wall in front of me. There was no door. My bed faced the door of the room that was always left open, and outside of the room was a white wall in the hallway. It created an illusion that there was no door at all. I almost cried. I thought I could never go out again. That was the way it was ever since. It was the first time that that happened to me. Since then, I've been experiencing this at least once every year, when I'm really stressed and preoccupied.

Four days inside a four-walled room. It had enough room to cater to human needs, but it felt specifically tiny during those days. Those were the days when there were too many things to think about. Those were the days that I do not want to experience ever again. But those days are the kind of days that I'm always having now and will always be having in the future. But the four-walled room that I resented took me to a reality that I've never been to. The reality that nothing ever stays the same and only I can change my life. It may be hard, but I can always grab tight on a pillow just for reassurance and enjoy the joyride.

War-Torn

Shanika Marie Lumayno

Pre-War

Imagine a field clutched by the hand of darkness. Pools of blood paint the scenery, as if the sky was tinged with crimson. Sometimes, the darkness is suffocating; other times, the red feels like too much sun on my skin. And instead of a burn, it's an endless itch that cannot be scratched, and the red on my skin is the same as the red in the sky. This is what my head feels like: dark, bloody, and torn. But sometimes, the sky clears and the darkness loosens its fingers, and I am okay. This is what I imagine my head would look like if what I feel on nearly a daily basis was put into a picture.

The March

Mental health is important. This is what I've learned going through my six years in high school. The first year was terrible. I wasn't the type to hyperventilate and get panic attacks due to anxiety, but I did tend to vomit, and I couldn't get myself to eat properly. I found myself quickly losing weight, and that was the skinniest I've ever been in high school. This whole ordeal happened just because I was in a new environment, and traditional school was a huge adjustment from my usual Montessori and modular type. It scared me to death. How did I manage it? I told myself to suck it up, and in time, I was able to adjust. There wasn't much darkness in the first year, but my hands trembled and my legs were shaky.

War Cry

The second year was the easiest to get through. I found solace in people. My friends were my fellow soldiers in a battle we called "school." Bonds were made stronger than the French Barricades, and love ran deeper than any trench ever made. A lot happened that year. I found a family in the Glee Club and things were fine, until I had my first breakdown. I don't even remember why or how it happened, it just did and I found myself crying in the middle of class. It was also the same year my lack of appetite morphed into binge-eating. I guess this could be the part where the beginnings of a war cry could be heard. My mind was slowly turning on my body. It was an ambush on myself by *myself*, and I feel like that's the worst type to go through. Obviously, it didn't do anything for my mental health.

Bloodshed

The third year was the year I developed depression. It was caused by my very first heartbreak. On the first day of class, I found out my best friend had enrolled in another school. She didn't even say goodbye. And I found myself wondering if I was really that disposable, replaceable, and forgettable. What could be so wrong with me that it made someone leave? Every insecurity clawed its way up to the surface, and the war cry was no longer a simple echo through an abandoned field. No, it was deafening. The darkness had crept in and blood had been shed. For every reason I came up with why she left, there was a bullet that went right through me. And there were a lot of reasons. This was the year I used poetry as an outlet, the year I learned how to write down my feelings like scratching my pen into the paper. It looked a lot like I was scratching into my own arms; the scars were the words and the blood was the ink. It was a dark year, and the stronger-than-the-French Barricade of a bond took its first hit.

Darkness

The fourth year was a struggle! On top of preparing for senior high school, I had to deal with falling in love. It was terrible. I wrote poems after poems and songs after songs. It was a weird time for me. I think I lost a part of myself in the whirlwind of creativity and inspiration that first love brought with him. I don't think I will ever be as inspired as I was back then. And like everything that comes into this world, it has to end. I had my second heartbreak. It was equally as bloody and messy as the last one, except that I feel like there's a part of me that I'm never going to get back, and in its place is a seed of fear, planted there for every time I fall in love again. A warning to abandon all hope written on my heart that way soldiers write lines on their helmets. As expected, my depression got worse. I pushed people away, and that gave the darkness a chance to creep in, its fingers getting closer and closer to my mind. The Barricade took another hit. Although a war was raging inside my own head, the rest of my body felt like it was chained to my bed, and it was getting harder and harder to get out of it each day.

Down with the Barricades

Year number five brought about a new beginning. Wounds weren't fully healed and scars were yet to be formed, but it was a fresh start and this part of the battlefield was as clear as day. This year, I realized that anxiety was actually a thing for me. I didn't have it in the form that most people did, but I tended to shake so bad whenever something made me nervous. Sometimes, it was hard to swallow; other times, I was too aware of my own heartbeat. The war in my head raged on, and my body was still stuck to the bed. There was blood everywhere and the Barricades had finally collapsed on the bonds. I made new friends, but they turned out to be backstabbing spies from the enemy lines. There goes my third heartbreak. By the end of that year, my wounds from the previous one had healed, but new ones appeared all over my body, mind, and soul. The war seemed like it would never end.

War-Paint

The last year was just as amazing as it was painful. I managed to rebuild the broken Barricades and re-dig those trenches, but life had taken its toll on me. Another heartbreak was provided. My panic attacks got worse and all I could do was sit through them and suffer, while my own mind attacked itself. The darkness will always be there, ever-present. Sometimes, it loosens its grip on me and I am able to breathe, but only momentarily. I may look okay on the outside, smiling and talking to people like nothing is wrong, but on the inside, I am suffering. Countless breakdowns happened this year and the tears I shed could rival the blood that caused the sky to turn red.

Post-War

In the end, nothing happened. I didn't get any better. And I think that's the perfect representation of life. Miracles happen, but harsh realities are easier to accept and hold on to. No one gets better if they don't actually let themselves get better, and I never gave myself the chance to do that. Instead, I found distractions. The solace in these distractions was enough for me. Reading, painting, listening to music, writing, and being around with my beloved friends are enough for me. Not a single doctor can heal some years' worth of bullet wounds from each shot I took after every heartbreak I went through. But accepting what I have in hand can make things better, and the comfort of companionship is a relief. In an actual

war, when you cannot save yourself, your comrades
will.

A Beautiful Mistake

Janine Chilo Chin

Being a fruit of a mistake makes me feel sorry for my own existence. I'm like the wrong answer to a multiple-choice question in an exam. "If it weren't for me" thoughts have been haunting me for years, as if there is a thorn pierced through my heart. I have become emotionally attached to the belief that I'm a burden to people dear to me. That I'm guilty of robbing their dreams and cutting short their ambitions. Knowing this bitter reality that I'm someone they regret could have ruined my life completely. But I guess what prevents it from happening is the validation I've been longing for since I was young—that I'm worthy of their love and affection.

Being vulnerable yet trying to survive day by day takes so much courage. I always wanted to escape from reality and break away from such a sickening cycle. Although bruises of the past do not feel real anymore, the scars have stayed in good days and it feels like I'm still trapped. This cage I'm in is suffocating every bit of my spirit. Sometimes, it also feels that I'm hiding under tables, waiting for the earthquake to subside. Other times, I'm holding my breath underwater for a long time until the fire dies down. But who is really to blame?

Living in a superficial and materialistic world as a child with big dreams made me feel like I was stuck inside an aquarium when all I was daydreaming about was to reach the vast and infinite ocean. I have learned from a very young age that dreams are a luxury. I was only wishing for a happy and safe home, that's all. What was ordinary for others could be special for me. As the first-born child, I couldn't ask for those fancy Christmas decors because we could barely make ends meet. Thus, I resorted to selling candies and snacks to earn enough money and buy us a Christmas tree. Family outings on weekends, a refrigerator filled with food, blowing candles on surprise birthday parties, gifts on Christmas eve—these were only fantasies. I couldn't resist jealousy from creeping through my veins.

It felt as though my ears were bleeding from listening to hurtful words, and I couldn't even hear my own voice. People around me started to create their perceptions about my silence. I used to get bullied a lot as a child because I was very quiet, and whenever I tried to talk, it's barely audible. I was teased with "*Sing along pula'g ilong*" (Sing along, red-nosed one) because I used to turn red whenever I tried speaking in class. I thought that time it would've been so nice having someone who would ask me how my day was. Someone that I could run to for shelter. My refuge. My sanctuary.

Until a boy my age came along. He offered me his Hi-Ro biscuit and Zest-O juice when I was crying in a corner of the room. He became my very first real friend. I believed he was an angel sent to me before he ran out of time and had to return to heaven. He knew me too well. He listened to the song "Imagine me Without You" a lot of times. Maybe he was trying to tell me something. He loved the universe so much that he talked about it for hours whenever we had our simple picnics every Friday. His mere presence brightened up my gloomy days. He was the person who made me feel like it was safe to smile. He inspired me to be better and proved to me that I was worthy of the chance to live.

I became motivated to study harder so special people in my life can be proud of me. All my efforts didn't go in vain. I became the salutatorian of our batch back in 2012. On our graduation day, I searched for *them*, people dear to me, among the crowd, but they weren't there. I marched alone still hoping that they would appear beside me. As I got on the stage to deliver my speech, I saw one of them rushing, finding *her* way out of the crowd. She looked so happy and proud seeing the medals, ribbons and certificates I received. She apologized for being late saying that *they* were too busy preparing for the party in celebration of my achievement.

When we arrived, I caught *him* boasting to others about me being smart. He was saying how proud he was. I couldn't help but feel embarrassed yet touched at the same time. And it was then that a realization struck me. Yes, life must have been cruel to them, but they have sacrificed so much for me. The adult in me sees where they are coming from even though the child forever trapped inside of me is beyond repair to the point that she won't ever forget all those painful memories. And I am not sure if that is okay. Maybe it is wishful thinking to believe that I am a life of purpose and not a life that shouldn't have existed in the first place. Would it make me feel less unwanted if someone had told me once that even if I was a mistake, at least I was a beautiful one?

I'm still waiting for *them* to say this. Or maybe they don't have to. I just have to feel it.

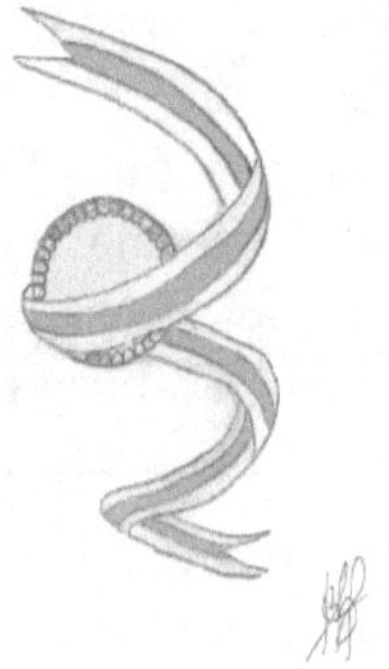

Wayward Currents

Pamela Denise Ceciban

The familiar feeling of nausea and sadness hit the pit of my stomach once again as we drove towards Mactan Cebu International Airport for the nth time to accompany my dad in going back overseas to work. It was very tiring. The traffic in Mandaue and Lapu-Lapu made the journey much worse. It occurred to me that all of these seemed too familiar. Somehow, I became nostalgic over the past years.

My mother told me that when I was four, my dad was in Saudi Arabia for the whole two years, so when he got back, I didn't know who he was. I'd cry if he took me away from my mom. My dad said that that was the most painful heartbreak he has experienced—going overseas to work, then coming back home to a child who did not have even the slightest hint of who he was.

When I was six, he went to Trinidad and Tobago to work as a waiter. The job that I took for granted was what my father did for a living. During my formative years, I never felt close to him. He was never around, and I always saw him as someone who just helped my mom in our financial needs, as cruel as it may sound. But I sent him e-mails, telling him that he should take care of himself, because after all, he took care of all of us.

When I was ten, he came home. And I didn't know why, but at that time, I hated his guts. Maybe because after all the years that he was gone, there he was, coming home. When someone was on the other side of the world, you never really knew who they truly were. Everybody loved him. But I didn't know who he was. I never had my dad around when I graduated pre-school. He wasn't there when I graduated from grade school, either. But my mom never failed to remind me why he wasn't there, why he had to leave us for such long periods of time. And I understood why. Or did I? But that didn't stop me from missing him and wondering how it feels like to have your dad around the house and for anything. The only dad I knew was on the computer screen.

Then my teenage years came. I learned to appreciate him more. He started going home every 10 months for a vacation. We grew closer to each other and I realized that I somehow got most of my mannerisms and the way I think things through from him. I also found out that we resemble the way he sees life and the way I see it. We have way many more similarities than I thought. He told me about all the troubles he got into while he was still a teenager like me. We laughed so hard because I was facing all kinds of trouble, too, but in a lesser gravity compared to his. Be it at school, family problems, or love problems.

Because of our life-talks and the laughter we shared, I realized that the purest kind of love is the kind of love that does not ask for anything in return.

Just the one that asks you to do good in life and to always take care of yourself. Because of my dad, I have learned what true love means and what my family means to me. Now I understand why poetry, love stories, and fairy tales were made. When you feel loved, everything in the world aligns, and that nothing in the world can harm you.

My dad started telling us how we should always take care of each other. It felt like each word had strings that tugged me into reality that I had to, once again, say goodbye to my father. The day felt longer and longer as I couldn't stop thinking and worrying what dad had to face just for us to have a proper meal on our table three times a day and to send us to a prestigious school. Just thinking that my dad will have to face wayward currents and have his other foot dug into the grave makes my chest thump, as if a time bomb kept ticking and ticking. When we arrived at the airport, I tried hard to stop my tears from falling because I didn't want to burden him with the thought that the last time he saw me was *me* with a pool of tears in my eyes. As we parted ways, I left my heart with my dad, because wherever he is in the world, I am there, too.

Dead Leaves

Matiz Erika Lumapas

I used to like being messy. I guess being unorganized will always be a part of who I am. The desk in my room that should have been clear so I could do my homework was always flooded with empty water bottles, scratch papers, and Post-it notes and other useless and nasty things I can think of. My floor was a total mess, too, most especially under my bed. It seemed like it's eating anything entering my room. It consumed pencils, slippers, sandals, socks, and shoes. My shelf overflowed with containers: hair bands, candies, mints, coins, earrings. I couldn't always see these things, but I always knew where to find them, placed somewhere on a shelf. Like old friends in a phone book, I thought that someday I would find all the loose strings and tie them together.

One uneventful day, I had random thoughts about random things and had come to think about the people I used to consider as my friends. It made me think, "Do they still think of me as their friend? I can't really recall any of my 'former' friends cutting ties with me." I had also wondered why I don't communicate with them anymore. "Maybe because all of us grow and mature, and we learn to pick people to connect with wisely," I told myself. After contemplating, I felt my insides begin to itch—well, that's how I described it. I tried taking a shower, scrubbing myself with the bar of soap aggressively. I brushed my hair and my teeth, but I didn't feel any cleaner. I checked my social media accounts, which were empty at that time. I tried to entertain myself by watching random videos on YouTube, but to no avail.

I went downstairs and found my brother playing video games, my mom in the kitchen preparing our lunch—everyone was in their right place. I told my mom that something didn't feel right, and she suggested that for once I should clean my room. The thought itself made me feel sick. I went upstairs to avoid another sermon from my mother, feeling so overwhelmed that I might as well have been swimming without a life vest in the middle of the Pacific Ocean. When I opened the door to my bedroom, everything was in its usual messy arrangement. Water bottles that had been there for almost a week, used clothes scattered on my bed, my underwear hung lifelessly from my doorknob. My blanket remained crumpled and cold across my bed, molded by the twists and turns of the previous night. My room appeared like a dumpsite. What a horrific view!

I stood in the middle of the grubby room, breathing in the dusty air that I had become so used to. In the silence of that moment, I thought again of the people that I used to be close with. While I was deep in my thoughts, a single name kept running across my mind. And that name was none other than Janny.

Janny and I have been friends since we were four years old. I consider her as my closest friend. I can still remember our favorite thing to do every day—popping the bougainvillea leaves. The popping sounds of the leaves were very entertaining, well, at least for us. We used to be very close to the point that we were almost inseparable. But that was just almost. Janny and her family migrated to New Zealand when we were nine. I can still remember being upset about it. I had so many worries running through my mind since my closest friend was going somewhere thousands of miles away without me. I didn't know how to contact Janny since I was too young for social media. So basically, a year went by, but Janny and I didn't talk to each other, not even once. After almost two years, Janny and her family decided to spend a two-week summer vacation here in Cebu.

One day, I was with my mother buying some groceries when I coincidentally ran into Janny and her mom. I didn't know what to do or say. It felt like I was being dipped in ice cold water. I didn't know what had changed but the Janny standing right in front of me was definitely not the Janny I used to know. It was obvious that both of us were feeling uncomfortable and were reluctant to greet first. It took a few seconds until Janny's mom broke the awkward silence between me and Janny. "I can see that you've grown a lot since the last time I saw you. How have you been, '*day*?" Janny's mom asked. My mind was panicking that my only response was a nod and an awkward smile. Janny and I didn't even talk to each other, but instead, we were avoiding each other's glances. Both of our parents bid their goodbyes and again I responded with a nod and an awkward smile.

When we got home, I had mixed emotions. I felt sad, intrigued, and slightly annoyed. It took me some days to forget that encounter. After two weeks, I heard from my mom that Janny and her family had already flown back to New Zealand.

Years passed. I turned 12 years old. I decided to create a Facebook account. I immediately added those people I knew. I also searched for Janny's Facebook and sent her a friend request. But days, weeks, months and even a year passed. Janny still didn't accept my friend request. I canceled my friend request as a realization struck me. "Maybe things have really changed for both of us." As I thought about my past memories with Janny, reality woke me up as I felt an itchy sensation in my arm and saw an ant biting me. That's when my brain registered that I was in a dusty and messy room. I plunged deep with my thoughts. For some unknown reason, I suddenly felt pity for everything in my room that I had buried, never to be seen again.

Lost items I had blocked out for years made their way back into my mind: my first ever friction pen, posters of a boy band I used to love, and a pair of socks that I used to wear every time I went to school. I had an urge to dive under my bed and discover everything hidden in the dark depths of dust, and to climb up into the highest corners of my closet and recover items that had been mingling with the spider webs. The innocent piles were growing higher and higher until they looked tarrying in my eyes. It's as if the spiders were threatening to swallow me whole. I had to get rid of them.

And so I started cleaning up.

In a box buried under old books, I found a picture and a letter that Janny had written to me during my seventh birthday. I had totally forgotten about this letter. I suddenly remembered the fun of running naked through a cold hose with Janny and my cousins, and the meaty smell of barbecue that we used to make every Sunday. I sat, holding the picture, not minding the rest of the mess around me. It felt like I was in the middle of a storm, but I sat there and studied the picture until I had memorized every detail in the photograph. I felt so emotional, and it's the sad type of being emotional. As I continued to clean my room, I walked over to the drawer and found a friendship bracelet that my childhood best friend, Janny of course, gave me before they moved to New Zealand.

I stared at the bracelet realizing that I hadn't spoken to her in years. The next day I tried adding her again on Facebook, with the hopes of being able to talk to her again for the first time in seven years. I was 12 years old when I tried adding her for the first time on Facebook and I was already 16 on my second attempt. But just like the first time, she didn't even bother to accept my request. I also sent her a message request, but I received no response. I had lost so many precious childhood memories over time, letting them slip through my fingers like grains of sand. That's when I realized that my friendship with Janny turned out to be like the leaves of bougainvillea. Our friendship just withered without us realizing it.

But I've also come to understand that life is too short. Things happen for a reason. Everything that happens in life is for a valid reason. People come in and out of our lives, and that is another reason. We have our own separate journeys in life. The most important people are those who we take with us in that journey and who we connect with. Now, I'm 18, still waiting for Janny to respond to my message, or perhaps accept my Facebook friend request.

"We count our pristine moments
As in lucid dream"

Edith Tiempo, *"The Third Hand"*

About the Writers & Illustrators

Kyla Sophia Abatayo (b. Talisay City, Cebu, 1999; illustrator), is a homebody that loves to draw and read books during her free time. She's a Disney and Horror movie enthusiast and likes visuals that keeps the thrill inside the four corners of her room. Her favorites in this great green earth are her three dogs, the Pixar film *Ratatouille*, and her best friend Vanessa Tan. (*illustrations: p. 37, 43, and 49*)

Kate Eloiza Alimpolos (b. San Fernando, Cebu, 1999; writer) has been and still is a fan of reading fairy tales for she believes that they can provide an escape into a world where dreams do come true. She thinks that if one wants something to happen in life, he or she should keep dreaming and striving for it. She is an open-minded and a free-spirited person—the kind who goes with the flow of life. She is an adventurer and lives by the rule that life begins at the end of your comfort zone.

Karen Claire Belocura (b. Cebu City, 1999; writer) is an active member of the Student Catholic Action of the Philippines. She is an avid fan of Korean Pop groups and artists, particularly Gfriend, Akdong Musician, Red Velvet, and IU. She also loves Korean Dramas such as *Shining Inheritance, Moon Lovers: Scarlet*

Heart Ryeo, and *Pinocchio*. God is her life, and her family is her source of strength.

Lance Roi Catadman (b. Lawaan, Talisay City, 1999; writer) was the Sports Editor of The Josenian Premier, the student publication of the SHS Department of the University of San Jose-Recoletos. He is a music creator who has his own home recording studio where he records his own composed songs. He is a Pokémaniac and traveler. He loves to lose himself deep into his thoughts and to learn more about the world. He is a stoic and nihilist who indulges in the bigger picture and the future, still struggling to live in the moment's little details. For someone who found the world meaningless, he found a girlfriend who shows him what a life full of meaning is.

Pamela Denise Ceciban (b. Cebu City, 1999; writer) is passionate about writing believing that it is the best way to express herself. She was also a finalist during the 1st YAMOG Creative Writing Workshop in the Poetry Category. She loves movies, and her favorite genres are sci-fi and horror. She dislikes speaking in public. Randomness runs in her veins, but at the same time, she's probably the most indecisive person one may ever know.

Janine Chilo Chin (b. Maigo, Lanao del Norte, 2000; writer) is currently staying in Cebu for her studies. She loves reading novels, playing musical instruments, and painting. She writes songs, poems, and other literary genres. She craves adventures so she travels a lot. She has a wide and deep imagination. She tends to get lost in her own train of thoughts and sometimes, she seems to be out of this world.

Devey Joy Gaviola (b. Lapu-Lapu City, Cebu, 1999; writer) lives her life going back and forth to her hometown and her family's current residence in Lapu-Lapu City. She is an amateur writer, a wannabe dancer and a frustrated singer. But on usual days, she is just like anybody else. She loves watching sunsets on the beach and the city lights. She is a fan of K-Pop, theatrical and classical music.

Jeanne Ross Heredia (b. Bulacao, Cebu City, 2000; writer) is an enthusiast of the arts who loves to go on adventures through reading, writing, and traveling. Jeanne dreams of exploring and experiencing great places and people where she can dedicate her poetry. She wakes up every day with a fresh and better perspective in life, and always looks forward to new adventures that tomorrow may bring.

Matiz Erika Lumapas (b. Pardo, Cebu City, 1999; writer) is very fond of animals and aspires to become a veterinarian in the future. She has two dogs that she treats like a family. She is a homebody and a wanderlust altogether. She enjoys mountaineering, kayaking, trekking, and camping. She prefers books to movies because she believes that movies ruin the storyline and the plot in books. She takes pleasure in reading Stephen King's works for she describes herself as a "thrill seeker." She loves watching the sea, sunset and all things aesthetic. She enjoys what this world has to offer her as she continues to ride with the waves of life.

Shanika Lumayno (b. Bulacao, Cebu City, 1999; writer and illustrator) loves all forms of art, particularly music, illustrative art, and literature. She's been a member of various choirs since her elementary days and her favorite musical is Lin Manuel-Miranda's masterpiece, *Hamilton*. She's also very into films and series, particularly the fantasy genre. A couple of her favorite films are *The Grand Budapest Hotel*, *Moana*, *The Greatest Showman*, *Marvel Movies*, *The Harry Potter Series*, and *The Age of Adaline*. Shanika loves hugs, dogs, the color gray, analogies, and metaphors. (*illustrations: p. 31, 72, and 84*)

Brenzy Kaye Maquilan (b. Minglanilla, Cebu, 2000; writer and illustrator) is an aspiring artist, singer, dancer, writer and a certified foodie. She is a regular teenager and an utterly awkward person. She lives for the love of art and is passionate about finding beauty in the oddest things. She is madly in love with creating, decorating, and inventing out of scrap. She hates rules and thinks that they restrict a person's creativity. She loves to work things her way and prefers working low-key. She can only love a few people and things, but when she does, she loves fiercely—no less and no in-between. (*illustrations: p. 88 and 92*)

Robert John Medida (b. Boljoon, Cebu, 1999; writer) was a student writer in his previous school. He is passionate about watching and reading news every morning and before bedtime. He idolizes TV news personalities most especially. He prefers to be in a crowd rather than being alone. Jokes and parodies from YouTube are his therapy. He is a wanderer and a movie enthusiast who does not want a happy ending especially in romantic films as he is not fond of dramatic resolutions.

Kci Saito (b. Cebu city, 1999; illustrator) always enjoys different art forms such as writing, music, and drawing. She grew up reading books, singing in choirs, and performing in school musicals. Right now, she is venturing into digital art, doing more drawing-related projects as she pursues her passion. She dreams to create a mark in this field as she continues exploring and improving her craft. (*illustrations: p. 18, 25, 56, 66, 78, and 98*)

106

Shymelissa Sunder (b. Minglanilla, Cebu, 1999; writer) loves reading dystopian novels while lounging on her couch. She feeds on BBC period dramas. As a petrolhead, no one would have guessed her to take a liking in writing. She loves chewing ice while watching a Formula 1 race and fangirling over Max Verstappen. She dreams to work in Formula 1 and at the same time travel the world.

Jewil Anne Tabiolo (b. Talisay City, Cebu, 1999; writer) was a student-leader in USJ-R. She owns four dogs. She finds comfort in the companion of books. J.K Rowling is her all-time favorite writer and Harry Potter is considered her childhood hero. She is a spontaneous and free-flowing person who doesn't want any part of her life figured out yet. She loves mystery, loves the unfamiliar, the unusual and the quirky. She aspires to achieve the state of inner peace and to find solace in the battlefield of life.

Samantha Tabotabo (Cebu City, 1999; writer) enjoys editing and exploring the wondrous art of visual media during her free time. She is fond of watching unsolved mystery cases and other movies. She is a silent girl with loud thoughts. Sam is interested in taking up AB Psychology since she's interested in learning and understanding human behavior.

About the Editor

Manu Avenido is a writer from Bohol, Philippines. His Cebuano short stories have appeared in the Bisaya Magazine and other anthologies. His memoir was included in the groundbreaking "The Bohol We Love" published by Anvil in 2017. Manu was a fellow to various regional and national writers' workshops. He is a recipient of the Palanca, the Lumbera, the Balacuit, and the SINULAT Awards. Holding a doctorate's degree in Literature and Communication, he has taught Literature and Creative Writing in Cebu before moving to Japan where he currently works as an English teacher. His maiden collection of Cebuano short stories with English translations is set to be published early next year.

www.ingramcontent.com/pod-product-compliance
Lightning Source LLC
LaVergne TN
LVHW091720190726
843493LV00001B/385